MW01504010

A ROSARY OF THE SEVEN SORROWS OF OUR LADY

Excerpts from

The Foot of the Cross

The Sorrows of Mary

By Fr. Frederick Faber

Edited by: Patricia M Mendoza

"We go out to meet Jesus in every action of the day; . . . we must rarely expect to meet Him except with a Cross . . . when we are in sorrow, He Himself "draws near and goes with" us, as He did with the disciples on the road to Emmaus. That is the privilege of sorrow."

Father Faber

TABLE OF CONTENTS

EDITOR'S NOTE

I was first drawn to the Seven Sorrows, or Seven Dolors, of the Blessed Virgin Mary when I was trying to heal from the death of our four-year-old son Martín who had succumbed to liver disease. In my search to understand my own loss, I came across *The Foot of the Cross, The Sorrows of Mary* by Fr. Frederick Faber. This book brought to life Our Lady's life of sorrow beyond anything else that I had read. Fr. Faber's writing is both poetic, which speaks to one's emotions, and yet is intellectual, providing concrete teaching into the theology of Mary as it relates to her "martyrdom" through the Seven Sorrows.

Devotion to Our Lady's Seven Sorrows dates back at least to the 1200s when the Servants of Mary, or the Servite Fathers, promoted the devotion through the Rosary of the Seven Sorrows.

This rosary is similar to the regular rosary however, it consists of seven sets of an Our Father and seven Hail Marys. Each set is for meditation upon each of her Seven Sorrows.

In a sermon once, a priest said that we should remember that we do not know the will of God unless He tells it to us, but in the case of the Seven Sorrows, He does tell us. He explained that while Our Lady was spared the pain of childbirth because she was without original sin, she came to bear a great pain when she accepted her spiritual motherhood of all of us at the foot of the Cross.

This great pain is foretold in the prophecy of Simeon, *"In thy own soul a sword shall pierce that out of many hearts, thoughts may be revealed."* According to the priest, these thoughts are the secret thoughts of our hearts – not the secret thoughts that we know and keep from others, but those thoughts within us of which we are not fully aware and therefore can cause us to sin. This explanation immediately resonated with me and gave me a deeper desire to explore Our Lady's sorrows.

This new insight surely relates to the first grace she promises to those who adopt this devotion; she promises peace in our families. Just imagine how the grace of knowing your weaknesses to sin can help us to control our tongues and rash judgments as spouses, parents, and siblings! Peace in the family that may have felt beyond our reach becomes attainable.

This little booklet then, is a collection of carefully chosen excerpts exclusively from *The Foot of the Cross* arranged into a text-based rosary to be used as a guided meditation on the Seven Dolors. So many of us fear we are too busy to tackle a lengthy book, but this devotional makes Fr. Faber's insights available to travel anywhere.

Therefore, the reader must understand that the text of this rosary was not written by me. *All of the words are directly taken from Fr. Faber's nearly 500-page volume.* The excerpts are not necessarily presented in the order in which he first published them over 160 years ago, however each Sorrow is annotated with corresponding page numbers for further reference.[1]

May these pearls from his gifted meditations enrich all who read them and encourage further contemplation of Our Lady's Seven Sorrows through *The Foot of the Cross.*

Patricia M. Mendoza

[1]Page references Fr. F. W. Faber, *The Foot of the Cross,* (London Oratory 1856)

Devotion to the Seven Dolors

The Blessed Virgin Mary passed on to St. Bridget that she will also grant to souls who honor her daily by saying seven Hail Mary's and meditating on her Seven Sorrows the following seven graces.

1. I will grant peace to their families.

2. They will be enlightened about the divine mysteries.

3. I will console them in their pains and I will accompany them in their work.

4. I will give them as much as they ask for as long as it does not oppose the adorable will of my divine Son or the sanctification of their souls.

5. I will defend them in their spiritual battles with the infernal enemy and I will protect them at every instant of their lives.

6. I will visibly help them at the moment of their death, they will see the face of their Mother.

7. I have obtained from my divine Son, that those who propagate this devotion to my tears and dolors, will be taken directly from this earthly life to eternal happiness since all their sins will be forgiven and my Son and I will be their eternal consolation and joy.

The Seven Dolors

1. On the large medal of the rosary:
    *   Make the sign of the cross.
    *   Read the Introduction to the Seven Dolors.
    *   Say the Apostle's Creed.
    *   Say the Act of Contrition.

2. For each of the next three beads, say a Hail Mary for an increase in faith, hope and charity, then a Glory Be.

3. Read the introduction to the First Dolor.
    On the first large bead: Say the Our Father. Then, for each of the next seven beads, read each of the numbered lines followed by a Hail Mary. Then, pray the Glory Be.

4. Read the introduction to the Second Dolor.
    On the second large bead: Say the Our Father. Then for each of the next seven beads, read each of the numbered lines followed by a Hail Mary. Then, pray the Glory Be.

5. Repeat this through each of the Seven Dolors.

6. Finish with the Hail Holy Queen, an Our Father, Hail Mary and Glory Be offered for the intentions of our Pope, and say three times: "Mary, who was conceived without sin and who suffered for us, pray for us."

7. Make a sign of the cross.

The Prayers

The Apostle's Creed

I believe in God, the Father Almighty, Creator of Heaven and earth; and in Jesus Christ, His only Son Our Lord, Who was conceived by the Holy Spirit, born of the Virgin Mary, suffered under Pontius Pilate, was crucified, died, and was buried. He descended into Hell; the third day He rose again from the dead; He ascended into Heaven, and sits at the right hand of God, the Father the Almighty; from thence He shall come to judge the living and the dead. I believe in the Holy Spirit, the holy Catholic Church, the communion of saints, the forgiveness of sins, the resurrection of the body and life everlasting. Amen.

The Our Father

Our Father, Who art in heaven, hallowed be Thy Name. Thy Kingdom come, Thy Will be done, on earth as it is in Heaven. Give us this day our daily bread. And forgive us our trespasses, as we forgive those who trespass against us. And lead us not into temptation, but deliver us from evil. Amen.

The Hail Mary

Hail Mary, Full of Grace, The Lord is with thee. Blessed art thou among women, and blessed is the fruit of thy womb, Jesus. Holy Mary, Mother of God, pray for us sinners now, and at the hour of our death. Amen.

The Glory Be

Glory be to the Father, and to the Son, and to the Holy Spirit. As it was in the beginning, is now, and ever shall be, world without end. Amen.

The Hail Holy Queen

Hail, holy Queen, Mother of mercy, our life, our sweetness and our hope. To thee do we cry, poor banished children of Eve. To thee do we send up our sighs, mourning and weeping in this valley of tears. Turn, then, O most gracious advocate, thine eyes of mercy toward us, and after this, our exile, show unto us the blessed fruit of thy womb, Jesus. O clement, O loving, O sweet Virgin Mary.

V. Pray for us, O holy Mother of God.
R. That we may be made worthy of the promises of Christ.

The Sorrows of Mary

Seven Sorrows Polyptych by Albrecht Dürer (1471 – 1528)

The Seven Dolors

The seven dolors are not seven separate mysteries, neither can we understand them if we look at them in that way. They have a unity of their own, and if we detach them from that unity, we miss their significance. They carry the whole of the three and thirty years along with them. Each of them depends for its truth, for its depth, for its intensity, for its peculiar character, on a certain portion of those years, inseparable from it. Jesus grows more beautiful. Grace rises proportionately in Mary's soul. The growth of grace is the growth of love.

The beauty of Jesus is inexhaustible. He is beautiful always, beautiful everywhere, in the disfigurement of the Passion as well as the splendor of the Resurrection, amid the horrors of the Scourging as well as amid the indescribable attractions of Bethlehem. But above all things, our Blessed Lord is beautiful in His Mother. If we love Him we must love her. We must know her in order to know Him.

Mary is continually changing, though it is only in one direction. Her life is an endless heavenward ascension. She is always increasing in holiness, because she is always increasing in love. She is always increasing in love, because Jesus is always increasing in beauty. Thus, each dolor found her at once less prepared and better prepared; less prepared because she loved Jesus more, and it was in Him that she suffered; more prepared, because stronger sanctity can carry heavier crosses.

Each dolor is a distinct sanctification to her, a renewal, a transfiguration, another degree of divine union. Then the process begins again. Grace and love accumulate once more, with an acceleration and a magnitude in proportion to her new height, until once more, in the counsels of God, they reach the point where another dolor comes to do its magnificent work. A life, with a broken heart almost from the first! This it was to be for the Mother of God.

And she had no suffering which was disassociated from the Passion of Jesus. We can make our sorrows in a measure like hers by continually uniting them to the sorrows of our Lord. If our sorrow comes from sin, of course it cannot be like Mary's sorrow; but it can be just as easily, just as acceptably, united with the passion of our Lord. He will not despise these offerings. Happy they, and true sons, whom our Father punishes in this life![2]

---

[2] Fr. F. W. Faber, *The Foot of the Cross* (London Oratory 1856) P.1, 94, 113, 232, 240

The Prophecy of Simeon

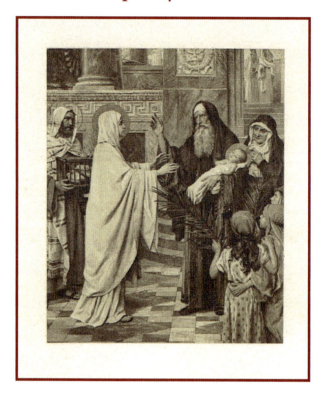

Forty days had gone since the angels sang at midnight. The roofs of the Holy City are in sight, with the glorious temple shining above all – to that temple, to His own temple, the visible Infant God was now going. Mary came to present her Child to God, and do for the Creator what no creature but herself could do, give Him a gift fully equal to Himself. And the greatest gift which we learn from this first sorrow of Mary, is that the highest use of God's gifts is to give them back to Him again.

Our Father . . .

1. There was the aged Simeon – the blossoms of the grave clustered thickly on his head.

Hail Mary . . .

2. He was willing heaven should be put off, if only he might see that sight on earth - the Christ!

Hail Mary . . .

3. Light thy heart at the fire of those little eyes – it is the Christ!

Hail Mary . . .

4. There is other music now for Mary's ear, the terrible music of dark prophecy which the Holy Ghost utters from His sanctuary in the old priest's heart.

Hail Mary . . .

5. "Behold, this Child is set for the fall, and for the resurrection of many in Israel; and for a sign which shall be contradicted. And thy own soul a sword shall pierce, that out of many hearts thoughts may be revealed." Lk 2:34-35

Hail Mary . . .

6. Since she left her home in December, how much has passed, but the sunset looks on Nazareth, gilding its white cottages as though all had gone on the same . . . Oh how cruel unchanging nature looks to a heart that has been changed in its own despair.

Hail Mary . . .

7. Earthly sorrows are the roots of heavenly joys – a cross is a crown begun.[3]

Hail Mary . . .

Glory be to the Father . . .

---

[3] Faber. P.81-8, 113

The Flight into Egypt

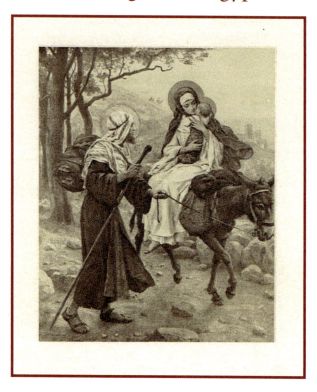

There was Mary with her Magnificat, instead of Miriam and her glorious seaside song; and another Joseph, greater and dearer far than that saintly patriarch of old, who had saved the lives of men by husbanding the bread of Egypt, whereas this new Joseph was to guard in the same Egypt the living Bread of everlasting life.

And fearfully, like stigmata upon the saints, upon Mary's ardent love, passed the many wounds of the Eternal Object of her love. She shuddered at the abyss of darkness, the capabilities of separation from God, . . . and a sort of sacred horror passed upon her . . . All the loves of her heart were crushed. Jesus was hated.

Our Father. . .

1. In the dead of night, the Lord appeared in sleep to Joseph, the keeper of heaven's best treasures on earth, and bade him rise, and take the Child and His Mother, and fly into Egypt.

Hail Mary . . .

2. Thus it was at once a sorrow to Joseph to convey fresh sadness to Mary, and to her to receive it from him.

Hail Mary . . .

3. The three kings had gone back to the east without telling Herod whether they had found the newborn king.

Hail Mary. . .

4. Tyranny, was not, however, to be so balked, and lest it miss its aim, involved all Bethlehem in blood by the massacre of the Innocents . . . what a concourse of wailing sounds rose to heaven from that narrow hilltop .

Hail Mary . . .

5. Mary took up her treasure, as He slept, and went forth with Joseph into cold starlight; for poverty has few preparations to make.

Hail Mary . . .

6. Terror and hardship, the wilderness and heathendom, were before her; and she confronted all with calm anguish of an already broken heart.

Hail Mary . . .

7. But as Jesus had come like God, so He went like God, unnoticed and unmissed.[4]

Hail Mary . . .

Glory be to the Father . . .

---

[4] Faber. P. 123, 131, 152, 154

The Three Days Loss

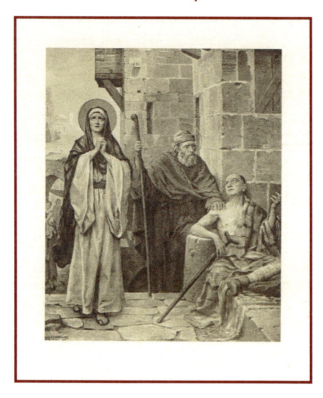

But all things were not always clear to Our Lady. As our Lord at seasons veiled the operations of His Sacred Heart from her sight, so sometimes the future was not present to her, nor the whole mystery of the present understood. So according to His will, our Blessed Mother little deemed that, while His Calvary was still years off, hers was close at hand.

Our Father...

1. He went up to Jerusalem at the Pasch, with Mary and Joseph, and according to the tradition, He went on foot.

Hail Mary . . .

2. But how the mystery deepens when between Joseph and Mary kneels down the Everlasting God . . . would the songs go on in heaven when the Incarnate Word prayed on earth?

Hail Mary . . .

3. But the end of the week... they left, the men by one gate, the women by another... an opportunity was also thus presented to our Blessed Lord to separate from them unperceived.

Hail Mary . . .

4. Mary went upon her journey... the Holy Ghost flooded her soul with unusual sweetness... her thoughts gently diverted from the absence of Jesus.

Hail Mary . . .

5. They were suddenly alone . . . . Joseph crushed to the very earth . . . an abyss had opened and a cold wind was rushing out of it which froze every sanctuary of Mary's soul as they made their search . . . two hearts in such consummate misery.

Hail Mary . . .

6. Had He withdrawn His wonted illumination from her heart forever? . . . Was she unworthy of Him? She knew she was. Had He left her?

Hail Mary . . .

7. Mary and Joseph go up to the temple . . . it is the voice of Jesus . . . the doctors are looking at Him with a combination of awe and pleasure . . . "Did you not know I must be about My Father's business?" Is the darkness gone? For the moment, He has thickened it by His words. [5]

Hail Mary . . .

Glory be to the Father . . .

---

[5] Faber. P. 178-9, 182-7, 194

Meeting Jesus with the Cross

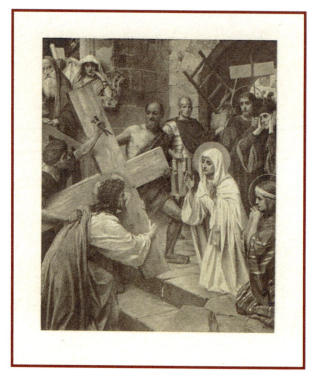

By miraculous grace the Blessed Mother assists in spirit at the Agony in the Garden, sees our Lord's heart unveiled throughout, and feels in herself, and according to her measure, a corresponding agony. She sees the treachery of Judas consummated, in spite of her intense prayers for that unhappy soul. Then the curtain falls; the vision grows dim; she is left for a while to the anguish of uncertainty.

Then with the brave, gentle Magdalene, Our Lady goes forth into the streets. She tries to gain admittance both to the houses of Annas and Caiaphus, but is repulsed, as she was at Bethlehem three and thirty years ago.

At all the horrors of the morning she is present. . . . She hears the sound of the scourging, and sees Him at the pillar, and the people around Him sprinkled with His blood.

Our dearest mother, brokenhearted, yet beaming, as with divine light in her tranquility . . . with Magdalene, and the apostle John, who, will lead her to the end of the street, where she can meet Jesus on His road to Calvary.

There was another aggravation of her grief in this dolor - the knowledge that the sight of her increased our Lord's sufferings. In the preceding dolor He had been, as it were, her executioner; now she was His.

Our Father . . .

1. The procession comes into sight; the tall horse of the centurion shows first, and leads the way.

Hail Mary . . .

2. As He draws nigh, the peace of her heart grows deeper. It could not help it; God was approaching, and peace went before Him.

Hail Mary . . .

3. He halts for a moment. He lifts the one hand that is free, and clears the blood from His eyes. Is it to see her? Rather, that she may see Him, He looks of sadness, His look of love.

Hail Mary . . .

4. He staggers, is overweighed by the burden of the ponderous Cross, and falls with a dull dead sound upon the street. She sees it. The God of heaven and earth is down.

Hail Mary . . .

5. Men surround Him, they kick Him, beat Him, swear horrible oaths at Him, drag Him up again with cruel ferocity. It is His third fall.

Hail Mary . . .

6. He is her babe of Bethlehem. She is helpless.

Hail Mary . . .

7. She cannot get near.[6]

Hail Mary . . .

Glory be to the Father. . .

---

[6] Faber. P. 243, 246-7, 250

The Crucifixion

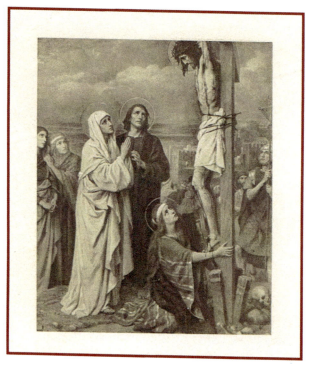

Our Lady comes to the Crucifixion a greater marvel of grace, a greater miracle of suffering, than when an hour ago she had met the cross-laden Jesus at the corner of the street. The soldiers have stripped Him of His vestments, from the shame of which stripping His Human Nature shrank inexpressibly. To His mother the indignity was a torture itself, and the unveiled sight of Her Son's Heart the while was a horror and a woe words cannot tell.

The soldiers' iniquity rose to the brim that very morning. And the breaking of Mary's heart was a portion of their iniquity. But at least over her heart Jesus was acknowledged King, and reigned supreme. So was it with the dear Magdalene and the ardent John, and as she thought of this, she looked upon them with a very glory of exceeding love. Is it that Jesus breaks the hearts over which He reigns, or that He comes of special choice to reign in broken hearts?

Mysteries, exceeding all mysteries that had ever been on earth were going on in His Heart. It had divine support, but divine consolation was carefully kept apart. The interior of that Heart was clearly disclosed to the mother's inward eye, and her heart participated in its suffering. Never did anyone so walk by faith, simple naked faith, as Mary did that day. There was faith enough to save a whole world in her single heart.

Our Father . . .

1. They have laid Him on the cross, a harder bed than the crib of Bethlehem in which He first was laid.

Hail Mary . . .

2. The soldiers supply the rough nail to the palm of His Hand, the Hand out of which the world's graces flow, and the first dull knock of the hammer is heard in the silence.

Hail Mary ...

3. The Magdalene and John hold their ears for the sound is unendurable; it is worse than if the iron hammer were falling on their living hearts. Mary hears it all.

Hail Mary . . .

4. She looked up to heaven. She could not speak. Words would have said nothing. The Father alone understood the suffering of that heart, now broken so many times.

Hail Mary . . .

5. Father! Forgive them for they know not what they do! When Our Lord breaks the silence, it is not about His mother, or the apostles, or Magdalene. It is for sinners, the worst of them.

Hail Mary . . .

6. . . . and the loud cry went out from the hilltop, hushing Mary's soul into an agony of silence, and the Head dropped toward her, and the Eye closed, and the Soul passed her.

Hail Mary . . .

7. And Mary stood beneath the cross a childless mother. The third hour was gone. [7]

Hail Mary . . .

Glory be to the Father . . .

---

[7] Faber. P. 289, 295, 297-8, 311

The Taking Down from the Cross

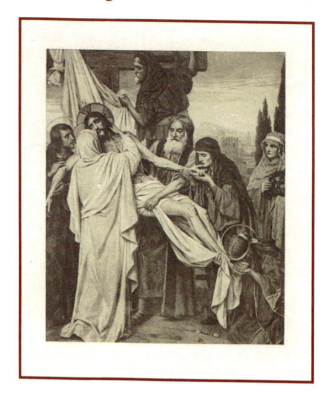

The darkness of the eclipse had passed away, and the true shades of evening were beginning to fall. The Soul has left her but she has the Body still. Immense as is the holiness of Mary's Immaculate Heart, sorrow can still find work to do . . .

This is the case with the Sixth Dolor, the Taking Down from the Cross. It is the grief of an accomplished sorrow, and in this respect, differs at once from the strain of a distressing anticipation, or the active struggle of a present misery . . .

Joseph touches the crown of thorns, and delicately loosens it from the Head of which it was fixed, disentangles it from the matted hair, and without daring to kiss it, passes it to Nicodemus, who reaches it to John, from whom Mary, sinking on her knees receives it with such devotion as no heart but hers could hold.

Our Father . . .

1. Mary is kneeling on the ground, her fingers stained with Blood. She stretches the clean linen cloth over her arms and holds them out to receive her Son.

Hail Mary . . .

2. Can she bear the weight? Which weight? The sorrow or the Body? It matters not. She can bear them both.

Hail Mary . . .

3. Mary prostrates herself in an agony of speechless adoration, and ... the Babe of Bethlehem is back again in His mother's lap.

Hail Mary . . .

4. She still fills the lifeless figure with the life of her own love.

Hail Mary . . .

5. Her grief was past nature's soothing. For her Flower had been cruelly gathered, and lay withered upon her knee.

Hail Mary . . .

6. With heroic effort she has bound the napkin around His Head, and folded the winding sheet over the sweet Face.

Hail Mary . . .

7. The very dead Body has been a light and a support. She has put out the light herself.[8]

Hail Mary . . .

Glory be to the Father . . .

---

[8] Faber. P. 344-5, 356, 360-64

The Burial of Jesus

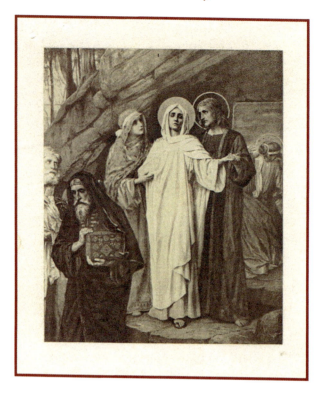

The shades of evening fall fast and silently round that mother, sitting at the foot of the Cross with the covered Head of her dead Son upon her lap. There is a divine light in the heart of Mary, more golden than that last lingering rim of departed sunset, that sun which seems so glad to set after the burden of such a day, and she is resting on it for a moment, before she girds up her whole nature to meet her seventh sorrow and her last.

When Mary sat on that hilltop, and enthroned the dead Christ upon her knees, she left an inexhaustible legacy of blessings behind her to all generations, with the condition of residence on the top of Calvary attached to their enjoyment. But the time has now come, and she signifies with calm self-collection to the disciples round to form the procession to the tomb.

Our Father . . .

1. With calm heroism, yet not without the direst martyrdom, Mary gave up the Treasure which lay across her lap.

Hail Mary . . .

2. There is that other Joseph, haunting thee with his sweet look of reverence and love through these last two mysteries of thy sorrow. He and Nicodemus will bear the burden, while John and Magdalen will go along with thee.

Hail Mary ...

3. There was grief enough to have darkened a whole world in Mary's single heart.

Hail Mary . . .

4. There was only one sacrifice she could make now . . . that Body which though it was dead was more than life to her.

Hail Mary . . .

5. The tomb of this new Joseph was to be to Him what the arms of the other Joseph had often been before, His resting-place a while, when Mary had to part with Him.

Hail Mary . . .

6. Mary enters the tomb with Joseph. Her hands arranged everything. How gently they lowered His Head into the tomb!   . . . on her knees she made her last act of adoration of that lifeless Body.

Hail Mary . . .

7. For Mary, his own mother, to be Christless, and on the night of such a day, - oh, the sorrow lies out dark before us, like the sea at night and we know no more! [9]

Hail Mary . . .

Glory be to the Father . . .

---

[9] Faber. P. 397-99, 402-5

The Compassion of Mary

At first we stood on the shore of Mary's sorrows and gazed upon them as one vast ocean. We then sounded, one after another, 7 abysses of that ocean, which the Church selected and presented to us. Now we look at her dolors again as one, but pouring their water through the Strait of Calvary into the mighty ocean of the Precious Blood.

This co-operation of our Blessed Lady is, therefore another summit from which we gain a fresh view of her magnificence. It is the grandest privilege of the creature to be a fellow laborer with the Creator, just as it will be our home and blessedness to enjoy His everlasting Sabbath.

But what is to be said of co-operating with Him in such a work as the redemption of the world and co-operating in it with such as efficacy, intimacy, and reality, nay, with a co-operation simply indispensable to its accomplishment? What an idea does it convey to us of immeasurable holiness! What gifts and graces does it not presuppose! What marvelous union with God does it not imply!

What then is the place which Our Lady's compassion holds in the purposes of God? This grandeur of co-operation in a great measure answers the question. Her dolors were not necessary for the redemption of the world, but in the counsels of God they were inseparable from it. They belong to the integrity of the Divine Plan; and they doubtless perform many functions in it which we are unable to apprehend, and which perhaps we do not so much as suspect.

According to God's ordinance, without shedding of blood there is no remission for sin. One of our Lord's infantine tears had enough in it of worth, of humiliation, of merit, and of satisfaction, to redeem the sins of all possible worlds. Yet as a matter of fact we were not redeemed by His tears, but only by His blood.

Hence Bethlehem was not necessary for our salvation, nor the worship of the three kings, nor the presentation in the temple, nor the Flight into Egypt, nor the disputing with the doctors. Nazareth was not necessary for our salvation, with all the beautiful mysteries of those 18 years of hidden life. The public ministry, with its three years of miracles, parables, sermons, conversions, and vocations of apostles, was not necessary to our salvation.

Indeed our Lord might have suffered as a child, or He might have come full grown like Adam, and simply suffered death at once. His blood was all that was absolutely necessary. But Bethlehem and Nazareth and Galilee belong to the integrity of the divine plan. They are not only congruent, and beautiful, insignificant, and full of teaching; but there are deeper mysteries in them, and a divine reality, simply because God planned it so.

So it was with Our Lady's dolors. Her maternity was indispensable to the Passion. Her dolors do not appear to be so. But they were an inevitable consequence of her maternity under the circumstances of the Fall. They take their place among the gospel mysteries. They rank with the mysteries of Bethlehem and Nazareth, not perhaps in their intrinsic importance, but in the relation in which they stand to the redemption of the world.

Indeed, we may be allowed to say that even in their intrinsic importance they might be compared with some of our Lord's own mysteries. For it is quite clear that His mysteries and hers cannot be divided off in this way? Are not her mysteries His, and His mysteries hers? Is not the Immaculate Conception the glory of His redeeming grace? Is not her purification as much His mystery as His own presentation? And in the case of the dolors, the union of the mother and the Son is greater than any other mystery. He is Himself her one dolor seven times repeated, seven times changed, seven times magnified.

The truth appears to be, that all the mysteries of Jesus and Mary were in God's design as one mystery. We cannot break it up, and divide and parcel it out, and classify the importance of its various mysteries. . . . . The whole of the Three and Thirty Years, and the Hearts of Jesus and Mary and all the mysteries of those years are tinctured with the Passion; yet outside the Passion itself, where are the colors deeper, and the traits more life like, than in the mother's dolors? Mary's Compassion was the Passion of Jesus as it was felt and realized in His Mother's Heart. [10]

[10] Faber. P. 455-9

Daily Meditation on Our Lady's Seven Sorrows

1. The Prophecy of Simeon -"And thy own soul a sword shall pierce, that out of many hearts thoughts may be revealed." Lk 2:34-35
Hail Mary . . .

2. The Flight into Egypt -Tyranny involved all Bethlehem in blood by the massacre of the Innocents . . . and Mary took up her treasure, as He slept, and went forth with Joseph into cold starlight; for poverty has few preparations to make.
Hail Mary . . .

3. The Three Days Loss - Mary and Joseph were suddenly alone. An abyss opened which froze every sanctuary of Mary's soul as they made their search.
Hail Mary . . .

4. Meeting Jesus with the Cross - Men surround Him, kick Him, beat Him, swear horrible oaths at Him. He is her Babe of Bethlehem. She cannot get near.
Hail Mary . . .

5. The Crucifixion - Mary looked up to heaven. The Father alone understood the suffering of that heart, now broken so many times, as she stood beneath the Cross a childless mother.
Hail Mary . . .

6. The Taking down from the Cross - Mary prostrates herself in an agony of speechless adoration, and the Babe of Bethlehem is back again in His mother's lap.
Hail Mary . . .

7. The Burial of Jesus - There was only one sacrifice Our Lady could make now. On her knees, she made her last act of adoration of that lifeless Body, which though it was dead, was more than life to her.
Hail Mary . . .

**Mary's Compassion was the Passion of Jesus
as it was felt and realized in His Mother's Heart**

Father Frederick Faber was born in England in 1814 and died in 1863 at the age of 49. He was first ordained a priest in the Church of England in 1836, and then traveled in Europe, specifically Rome where he became drawn to the practices and rituals of the Roman Catholic Church. He eventually found his way to the Church in 1846 having also been influenced by his close association with St. John Henry Newman.

Ordained as a Catholic priest in 1847, it is believed that Fr. Faber developed his devotion to the Blessed Virgin Mary during a near fatal illness. This led him to translate into English St. Louis de Montfort's, *True Devotion to Mary*. *The Foot of the Cross* is one of his eight major theological works. He was also an accomplished poet and hymnist with "*Faith of Our Fathers*" being his most notable hymn.